Day by day
with the love of God
Vol. 3

MY NEIGHBOUR
AS MYSELF

DOROTHY B. KING

With Foreword by Patience Strong

DENHOLM HOUSE PRESS
National Christian Education Council
Robert Denholm House
Nutfield, Surrey RH1 4HW

First published 1977

© Denholm House Press

ISBN 0 85213 163 1

DEDICATION
I dedicate this little book to
Mothers, whose love for their
children is of the utmost
importance for the well-being
of the whole world.

Cover Design : Donald Grey

Typeset by Surrey Graphics, Dorking

Printed by
Ebenezer Baylis & Son Ltd., Worcester

CONTENTS

FOREWORD

by Patience Strong

The trouble today with the world in general and with our own country in particular is that there are too few Dorothy Kings around to leaven the lump of materialism with the yeasty spirit of a religion with life in it, a religion that is both mystical and practical, active and contemplative: in short, the gospel as taught by our Lord himself.

The uncompromising rule of Divine priority runs like a golden thread through this helpful and inspired little book. If you do indeed love God with all your heart, soul and mind, how can you not love your neighbour? Love is the fulfilling of the law, wrote St. Paul, and he declared love to be greater than faith or hope.

The word love is one of the holy words of life, but in this unholy age it has become tarnished. It is now a blanket word covering every kind of affection. Failure to understand its true meaning has been partially responsible for bringing about the so-called permissive society, and what mischief that ambiguous term has bred!

The kind of love that this book is about is the love that gives and is costly, and it is no respecter of persons, for Christian love demands that we act and speak with charity even to those whom we may dislike. This love is a solvent, melting away all that is hard and unforgiving in human nature. Love one another, said Jesus.

Mrs. King's book is a treasure; a book to keep and a book to give.

PATIENCE STRONG

ACKNOWLEDGEMENTS

The author and publishers wish to thank the following for permission to use copyright material. Every effort has been made to trace the source of quotations and if any remain unacknowledged the necessary amendments will be made in subsequent editions.

Evangelical Sisterhood of Mary, No. 24 (From the song "I come ever singing" from *Well-Spring of Joy* by Basilea Schlink.)

Hodder & Stoughton Ltd., No. 6 (L.D. Weatherhead), No. 7 (Henry van Dyke), No. 13 (Samuel F. Pugh), — from *A Private House of Prayer*; No. 8 (S. Wurmbrand, *The Pastor's Wife*).

Methodist Publishing House, No. 5 (W.E. Sangster, The Pure in Heart), No. 23 (R.W. Callin, copyright of the Methodist Conference).

Psalms and Hymns Trust, London, No. 15 (W.Y. Fullerton).

St. Andrew Press, No. 29 (William Barclay).

The following have also kindly given their permission:

Miss Olive Luff (Nos. 1 and 11), Patience Strong (No. 1), Rev. Norman Povey (No. 2), Lionel C. Paull (No. 3), Mrs. Lena Papprill (No. 7), Mrs. Edith Buxton (No. 11), Rev. John W.R. Robinson (No. 16), John W. Newton (No. 28), Miss Mulfra Williams (No. 9), Father J. Fox (No. 19).

PREFACE

My compilation of texts, prayers and thoughts on the Great Commandment is now completed — Thou shalt love the Lord thy God with all thine heart, and with all thy soul and with all thy mind and with all thy strength, and thy neighbour as thyself.

I leave all I have done in God's hands, believing that he will use it in his service.

The last word in the Great Command is "thyself". We cannot really love others with all our heart, soul, mind and strength if we are not fit to do so. Therefore our bodies must be kept in as good condition as possible, also our minds and most certainly our spirits. Each one of us is precious in God's sight — he wants our best; and always we are in his care and love. This will be emphasised in Section One.

Section Two focuses our attention on the Bible, where the Great Command is found. I hope the passages of Scripture from our greatest treasure will help and inspire you.

I want specially to thank once again my friends Dr. Frank Cumbers and Mrs. Lena Papprill for their invaluable help, including the typing of the material.

God bless every reader.

Frinton-on-Sea,   DOROTHY B. KING
Essex.
1976

SECTION ONE — Living in Love

1. Divine Love

Thou shalt love the Lord thy God with all thine heart, and with all thy soul, and with all thy might. And these words, which I command thee this day, shall be in thine heart; and thou shalt teach them diligently unto thy children.

Deuteronomy 6: 5, 6, 7.

We praise Thee, O God, we acknowledge Thee to be the Lord.

All the earth doth worship Thee, the Father everlasting.

To Thee all angels cry aloud, the heavens, and all the powers therein. To Thee cherubin and seraphin continually do cry,

Holy, holy, holy Lord God of Sabaoth;

Heaven and earth are full of the majesty of Thy glory.

The glorious company of the apostles praise Thee.

The goodly fellowship of the prophets praise Thee.

The noble army of martyrs praise Thee.

The holy Church throughout all the world doth acknowledge Thee

The Father of an infinite majesty,

Thine honourable, true and only Son,

Also the Holy Ghost the Comforter.

From the Te Deum Laudamus

Jesus asks us each to love
With a love from heaven above. *Olive V. Luff*

In God's love we find an answer to the restless thought; and we find the peace for which our weary minds have sought. In the silence we are quietened by a touch divine when we bow our heads and say, 'Not my will, Lord, but Thine'.

Patience Strong

Lord God, fill us with Thy love and power so that it overflows to all those with whom we come in contact.

2. Neighbourly Love

'Thou shalt love thy neighbour as thyself.'

Matthew 19.19

When Jesus bids us 'Love thy neighbour as thyself' he is stating the Golden Rule in another way. He is saying to us, 'Treat others as you would like them to treat you'. The love of our neighbour is very important indeed. It is the very heart of Christian living. There may be some truth in the assertion that it is easier to love someone unknown to you who lives at the other end of the world than the family who lives next door. But if we are to follow this great commandment we must try to do both. These people next door ought to be able to find the Heavenly Friend through the way we care for them, and the poor and under-developed nations of the world must be our concern at all times. The essence of neighbour-liness is to *be there* whenever and wherever we are needed. In the words of Sydney Carter's moving song:
And the creed and the colour and the name won't matter.
WERE YOU THERE?

Norman Povey

O Brother man, fold to thy heart thy brother!
Where pity dwells, the peace of God is there;
To worship rightly is to love each other,
Each smile a hymn, each kindly deed a prayer.

J.G. Whittier

Lord, may we learn to love ourselves wisely and well, so that we may love our neighbours better, and more truly understand their difficulties, and know how they need thy love and ours. Love is the greatest need ... and by giving love we give ourselves.

3. His Gift

If we love one another, God dwelleth in us, and his love is perfected in us.

1 John 4:12

I tremble at the thought of a world without love. Listen to some of your friends talking. 'I love to watch the children play' — 'I love to watch the graceful flight of birds' — 'I love the fragrant scent of flowers'. So often friends tell us of their loves. But erase them all, and the thousand others I have no space to quote, and what have we left? A vast, dank, chasmed gloom! God knew this. It is why he created love when he created land, sea and man. He knew, for *God is Love.*

>   Dear God above,
>   How many loves hast Thou giv'n me?
>   It seems, my Lord, there may be three;
>   Yes, one of course is love for Thee;
>   And two, my selfish love of me;
>   My love for neighbours makes it three.
>
>   Dear God above,
>   How many loves hast Thou giv'n me?
>   Could it be one and not the three?
>   Love for my friends, yes that must be,
>   and love for God and then for me;
>   All just one love, my gift from Thee,
>   For God is Love.

Almighty God, how can we live without your love? How can we die without loving you? You gave ALL when you gave love. May your love be perfected in us, for God is love.

All by *Lionel C. Paull*

4. Faith

But ye, beloved, building up yourselves on your most holy faith, praying in the Holy Ghost, keep yourselves in the love of God.   *Jude 20:21*

'Faith is the secret of power — why?
Because it is trust in a principle or a person and by that trust the power of that principle or person is brought into play. Faith in God enables God to work in our life and that of others. But faith needs to be held. We have to hold on in spite of difficulty, Like Columbus sticking to his course and his faith when all seemed lost. But as we hold faith it holds us. Think of the motto:— 'I hold and am held'. As we trust, the Grace of God becomes more credible and real. Faith, which is at first experiment and venture, becomes experience and discovery.'

Source unknown

This is my Father's world. Oh let me ne'er forget
That tho' the wrong seem oft so strong
God is the ruler yet.

This is my Father's world. The battle is not done.
Jesus who died shall be satisfied
And heaven and earth be one.

Source unknown

Lord, increase our faith, that, relying on thee as thy children, we may trust where we cannot see, and hope where all seems doubtful, ever looking unto thee, as our Father who ordereth all things well: according to the word of thy Son, Jesus Christ our Lord.

Source unknown

5. Rejoice

Rejoice in the Lord alway: and again I say, Rejoice. Be careful for nothing; but in everything by prayer and supplication with thanksgiving let your requests be made known unto God.   *Philippians 4: 4, 6*

Rejoice today with one accord,
Sing out with exultation;
Rejoice and praise our mighty Lord,
Whose arm hath brought salvation;
His works of love proclaim
The greatness of His name;
For He is God alone,
Who hath His mercy shown;
Let all His saints adore Him.

H.W. Baker

The joy of the Lord is constant. Children may know it. It can be the strong stay of youth; the means by which the middle aged may bear the heat and burden of the day; the secret exultation of those who grow old ... Joy never satiates ... Joy rises to rise again ... Joy is deep. It bubbles from utter contentment. The smile is not only on the lips but in the eyes, and in the heart.

W.E. Sangster

Lord, in thee will we rejoice. Thou art so great that we cannot understand or comprehend thy great love for us and thy power. But we humbly come to thee full of thanksgiving, knowing that thou dost love each one of thy children everywhere, and we are always in thy loving care.

6. Praise

Praise ye the Lord. Praise ye the Lord from the heavens:
Praise him in the heights ... Kings of the earth, and all
people; princes, and all judges of the earth: both young
men, and maidens; old men, and children: let them
praise the name of the Lord: for his name alone is
excellent; his glory is above the earth and heaven ...
Praise ye the Lord.   *Psalm 148: 1, 11-14*

Each of us has something for which to praise and thank
God. Indeed it is a revealing thing to write down a list of
those things for which we should thank God.
We should adore Him for all He is in Himself — and as
we do so, we should call to mind His attributes and
remember His love, His splendour, His power, His
beauty, His wisdom, His holiness. Then we can thank
Him for the way He has led us and for all He has done for
us.   *Leslie D. Weatherhead*

To God be the glory! great things He hath done!
So loved He the world that He gave us His son;
Who yielded His life an atonement for sin,
And opened the Life gate that all may go in.
O come to the Father, through Jesus the Son:
And give Him the glory! great things He hath done!
                              Frances J. van Alstyne

Beloved Father, we praise and bless thee for thy care of
us, we thank thee for thy love for us, help us to be thy
true servants, to know thou art our companion and
guide.
Praise be to thee, O God.

7. Action

For we are labourers together with God.

1 Corinthians 3: 9

They who tread the path of labour
  follow where My feet have trod;
They who work without complaining
  do the holy will of God;
Nevermore thou needest seek Me;
  I am with thee everywhere;
Raise the stone, and thou shalt find Me;
  cleave the wood and I am there.

Henry van Dyke

Work can be very satisfying; we pray for powers equal to our tasks; work can hold the joy of creating and making things or the greater reward of serving people. It can give us the opportunity to use our own initiative and to turn disappointments into God's appointments. Work can help us to know the joy of comradeship. Never did the world so need men and women with a zeal for working, greeting each new day with expectancy and wonder and finding God in the daily routine.

Lena Papprill

Heavenly Father, help us to overcome our weaknesses; give us the zeal for working, and as we work we would remember and endeavour to help those without work. May all we do be as thou wouldst have us do.

Lena Papprill

8. Suffering

Blessed are they which are persecuted for righteousness' sake: for theirs is the kingdom of heaven.

Matthew 5: 10

One morning, I was in church, scrubbing the floor, when Marietha rushed in waving a postcard ... I turned the cheap little card over ... it was signed 'Vasile Georgescu' but Richard's handwriting was unmistakable. I knew that political prisoners might write only ten censored lines. What could he say after so many years, not knowing if his wife and family lived? This dear, long dreamed of message began:— 'Time and distance quench small love, but make a great love grow stronger...' In prison they had taken away Richard's name.
He was V.G. The guards weren't allowed to know his identity ... if the secret leaked out questions might be asked abroad. He had to vanish without trace ... that was 1948.

The Pastor's Wife, *Sabina Wurmbrand*

Love suffereth long ... beareth all things ... endureth all things. Love never faileth. *1 Corinthians 13: 4, 7, 8*

'The Lord executeth judgment for the oppressed' but he does it through courts and customs and through the intervention of those who have his love in their hearts.

Frances Willard

Lord, give us that love that will never die. The love strong as death. Thy love which endures all things and never faileth. We thank thee for thy powerful love for us thy children.

9. His Promise

When thou passest through the waters, I will be with thee; and through the rivers, they shall not overflow thee.

Isaiah 43: 2

August 4th 1941. Under King's Orders — destination unknown! as a member of the Q.A.M.N. S./R. I had boarded the ship which had to pass through dangerous waters to our base, near a battle-field where brave wounded men were in urgent need. Naturally, personal baggage was limited but with my Bible I had my loved, helpful little book, 'DAILY LIGHT', from which I recall reading on that memorable day Isaiah 43: 2. It would be quite impossible for me to express the power of those strengthening words — the definite promise of 'our dear Lord's Protection and Presence'. How it enabled one to be comforted and strengthened by the power of His Love in spite of the nearness of the enemy. We were on the water six weeks. It was three months before I received a letter posted by a dear friend in England immediately she knew I was leaving for 'Service Overseas'. She assured me of her constant daily prayers and she quoted Isaiah 43: 2. I took this as a confirmation, not only of our being united by our Heavenly Father's Love but of His Precious Promise; knowing the Divine Healer was there I was enabled to work with others, to give succour to the wounded and the dying, whatever their race or creed.

Mulfra Williams

Thy nature, gracious Lord, impart;
Come quickly from above,
Write Thy new name upon my heart,
Thy new, best name of LOVE.

Charles Wesley

10. Life

Ye shall observe to do therefore as the Lord your God hath commanded you: ye shall not turn aside to the right hand or to the left. Ye shall walk in all the way which the Lord your God hath commanded you, that ye may live, and that it may be well with you, and that ye may prolong your days in the land which ye shall possess.

Deuteronomy 5: 32, 33

Live your life while you have it. Life is a splendid gift. There is nothing small in it. For the greatest things grow by God's law out of the smallest. You must not fritter it away in 'fair purpose, erring act, inconstant will', but must make your thoughts, your words, your acts, all work to the same end, and that end not self but God. That is what we call character.

Florence Nightingale

Walk in the light: and thine shall be
  A path, though thorny, bright;
For God, by grace, shall dwell in thee,
  And God Himself is Light.

Bernard Barton

O God, who knowest us to be set in the midst of so many great dangers, that by reason of the frailty of our natures we cannot always stand upright, grant to us such strength and protection as may support us in all dangers and carry us through all temptations. Through Jesus Christ our Lord.

Book of Common Prayer

11. Living Water

The water that I shall give him shall be in him a well of
water springing up into everlasting life.

John 4:14

Someone asked me the other day: 'Edith, what is your
aim in life now?' I think I can explain it by a true story I
was told in Africa. Water had been laid on to a village
through a pipe. One day the water stopped. There was
none to be had for miles, so they started to dig and at last
they came to the main supply; there was no water there
so they started to clear the main, and suddenly a jet of
water shot into the air, and on top of it were two dirty
sacks!

God has only us through whom to pour His living water
to this thirsty world, and my aim in life is to keep that
channel clean and flowing. You can block God's channel
so that He cannot reach others. My aim is to live so that
God's rivers of living water can come to this parched
world around us. I will let Him use me as a channel.

Edith Buxton
(daughter of C.T. Studd)

What the world needs is God's Love,
Shining from Heaven above;
Channels God needs for His love to flow through
In blessings to others — What about you?

Olive V. Luff

*Dear Heavenly Father, grant us thy blessing as we face
the tasks of life; show us, dear Lord, what our life's work
is to be, quicken our hearts with thy love, and ever keep
our wills keen to serve thee, and our hands quick to help
our brothers in their need; through Jesus Christ our
Lord.*

12. His Call

He saith unto them, Follow me. *Matthew 4: 19*

On many occasions Jesus said these words but they are first mentioned in the Gospels, to Simon Peter and to Andrew his brother ... and they straightway left their nets and followed him. Jesus knew their potentialities, as he knows ours. Others see our outside. The Triune God knows what we have in us to become, and power for that will be given us. When a small girl at Sunday School I signed a card which I still keep in the first Bible given to me by my father; it is inscribed:

'By the grace of God I acknowledge Jesus Christ as my Saviour and Lord, and in his strength I will strive to serve and follow him.'

How glad I am that in my early years I made that promise and learnt of the love of God and of his Son Jesus Christ.

Four times I have been round the world on my own; now in my eighties, I want to advise everyone to 'Follow him'. Jesus has been with me every step of the way. I have often, alas! failed him but he has never failed me. To-day I am happy and at peace.

Down in the valley or upon the mountain steep,
Close beside my Saviour would my soul ever keep;
He will lead me safely in the path that He has trod,
Up to where they gather on the hills of God.
Follow! Follow! I would follow Jesus,
Anywhere, everywhere, I would follow on,
Follow! Follow! I would follow Jesus,
Everywhere He leads me I would follow on.
W.O. Cushing

Thy love and guidance have never failed me, dear Lord.

13. Eternal

Lo, I am with you alway, even unto the end of the world.
Matthew 28: 20

Remember, when we think of God, that he is ever present and knows our every thought, when we are cast down he will uplift us — when we are happy and full of joy he shares our happiness — when we are weak he will give us strength to carry on. Joy! Hallelujah! Always we can rely on his love and care; sometimes we feel he has forsaken us — our prayers seem unanswered but he is with us, and in faith we must trust him and not be afraid for we are ever in his loving care.

I am not alone
By night,
Or by day,
Or by circumstance;
Neither in the silence,
Nor in the city's roar;
Nor as I lie
At the door of death,
or stand on the
Threshold
Of a new life;
For Thou art with me,
Bearing me up,
Giving me strength,
Luring me on.
I am not alone;
Thou hast been,
Thou wilt be,
Thou art
With me,
Lo, I am always in
  Thy care.   Amen.
Samuel F. Pugh

Dear Lord, make me worthy of thy wonderful love and care, that I may share it with others; in quietness and confidence I come to thee in perfect trust; take me, use me wherever thou wilt, filled with thy Holy Spirit and abiding eternally in thy love. Accept, dear Father, my humble, thankful heart.

14. The Sower

A sower went out to sow his seed: and as he sowed some fell by the wayside; and it was trodden down, and the fowls of the air devoured it. And some fell upon a rock; and as soon as it was sprung up, it withered away, because it lacked moisture. And some fell among thorns; and the thorns sprang up with it, and choked it. And other fell on good ground, and sprang up, and bare fruit a hundred-fold ... He that hath ears to hear, let him hear.

Luke 8: 5-8

My gratitude for teachers who never lost heart is only darkened by the knowledge that I was never able to tell all of them, in time, that I had come to be grateful. The good seed grows secretly, silently, and often so slowly that the sower has gone before the shoot has grown grain in its turn. None of us, not even a wise and dedicated teacher, is competent to judge what seed is wasted and which will take root.

Sid Chaplin

Sow a thought and reap a deed,
Sow a deed and reap a habit,
Sow a habit and reap a character,
Sow a character and reap a destiny.

Source unknown

Lord, may we sow seeds of blessing around us wherever we go. Fill our hearts with thy wonderful love, we beseech thee, so that flowers of joy may grow within us, and cheer and bless those with whom we come into contact. Thank you, dear Lord.

15. Praise the Lord

Let everything that hath breath praise the Lord. Praise ye the Lord.

Psalm 150: 6

I cannot tell why He, whom angels worship,
Should set His love upon the sons of men,
Or why, as Shepherd, He should seek the wanderers,
To bring them back, they know not how or when,
But this I know, that He was born of Mary,
When Bethlehem's manger was His only home,
And that He lived at Nazareth and laboured,
And so the Saviour, Saviour of the world, is come.

I cannot tell how all the lands shall worship,
When, at His bidding, every storm is stilled,
Or who can say how great the jubilation
When all the hearts of men with love are filled.
But this I know, the skies will thrill with rapture,
And myriad, myriad human voices sing,
And earth to heaven, and heaven to earth will answer:
At last the Saviour, Saviour of the world, is King!

W. Y. Fullerton

O for a thousand tongues to sing
My great Redeemer's praise,
The glories of my God and King,
The triumphs of His grace!

Charles Wesley

Let us in life, in death, Thy steadfast truth declare, and publish with our latest breath Thy love and guardian care.   *Paulus Gerhardt, tr. by John Wesley*

16. Discipleship

If the prophet had bid thee do some great thing,
wouldest thou not have done it?   *2 Kings 5: 13*

Naaman, captain of the host of the King of Syria, was a
mighty man of valour, but he was a leper. Elisha sent a
messenger to him saying, 'Go and wash in the Jordan
seven times'. But Naaman was angry. 'Are not Abana
and Pharpar better than all the rivers of Israel?' His
servants came near and said, 'My father, if the prophet
had bid thee do some great thing, wouldest thou not have
done it?' Naaman is insulted. His position as captain of
Syria's army should command more attention. He could
put military power at the direction of this religious
prophet. His illness demands more potent remedies. He
waits to do 'some great thing' and is in danger of missing
the cure altogether. We can, like Wesley, be in danger of
missing God's salvation because we wait for 'some great
thing' instead of trusting in Jesus and his cross.

We can miss the opportunity for service by looking for
'some great thing' when God is calling us to humbler
avenues of discipleship. Thank God for the people in our
churches who do not wait for 'some great thing' but get
on with the tasks that confront us now.

John W.R. Robinson

I am trusting Thee, Lord Jesus, trusting only Thee,
Trusting Thee for full salvation, great and free.

F.R. Havergal

17. Prayer

For I, the Lord thy God will hold thy right hand, saying unto thee, Fear not; I will help thee.   *Isaiah 41: 13*

Dr. Coggan, Archbishop of Canterbury, speaking at a Press Conference on October 16th, 1975, before a series of television and radio appearances, which it was hoped would reach every home, urged individual sacrifices, discipline and responsibility of work.

'I want to speak not only to members of the churches,' he said, 'but to all those who are concerned for the welfare of our nation at a time when many thoughtful people feel that we are drifting towards chaos. Many are realizing that a materialistic answer is no real answer at all. There are moral and spiritual issues at stake.

'I believe that the only creed that makes sense is: "GOD FIRST — OTHERS NEXT — SELF LAST". I see this worked out in the person and teaching of Jesus Christ. He has shown us the Way — he gives us the power to follow it.'

> Great King of nations, hear our prayer,
>   while at Thy feet we fall,
> And humbly with united cry
>   to Thee for mercy call.
>
> *J.H. Gurney*

God bless our nation. Guide our leaders. Give us Your power that we may live cheerfully, care for each other, and be just in all we do.

A prayer sent out by Dr. Coggan as a national prayer, October 1975

18. Love

Let all you do be done in love.

1 Corinthians 16: 14 (Moffatt)

When we love, we offer the gift of ourselves, and the gift must be worth offering. The man who loves is always seeking to give, particularly to give himself. We must give not only what we have but what we are. In the interest of love we must maintain a self that is worth imparting.

When we love, our life has two foci. Our personal life and the life of others. Love's sympathy gives us the key to the hearts of others, so that we may become sharers of their life, and we rejoice with them that rejoice and weep with them that weep.

Darlington Methodist Circuit Magazine 1928 (abridged)

King of Glory, King of Peace, I will love Thee;
And that love may never cease, I will move Thee.
Wherefore with my utmost art I will sing Thee,
And the cream of all my heart I will bring Thee.
Seven whole days, not one in seven, I will praise Thee;
In my heart, though not in heaven, I can raise Thee.

George Herbert

Our most loving Father, grant that we may not so much seek to be loved, as to love; for it is in giving that we receive. Lift our thoughts up to heaven and strengthen us by thy Holy Spirit that we may become co-workers with thee.

19. Unselfishness

And this is love, that we walk after his commandments.

2 John 6

The best kind of happiness on earth is when we lose ourselves in our care for another or others. Yet we are still on earth and we may get overworked and forget ourselves in the wrong way and become not helpful but irritable — and so less lovable — unless the time has come for us to practise the 'Greater Love' which transcends all regard for self. We must neither be anxious about our self-perfection, nor must we be careless about our health.

Think of a violinist, a great artist; think of the care he takes of his instrument; how he protects it from damp, from extremes of heat and cold ... so do you look after this precious instrument which is yourself. But first look at it; look at it in the mirror of the mind, with the aid, if you are fortunate, of a friend or a beloved spouse. Look at yourself in this mirror of the mind where you can see your laziness, or your anxiety, or your indulgence or your pride. See what you might have been if you had loved yourself, your body and mind, in the right way.

Father J. Fox

O Divine Master, grant that
I may not so much seek
To be consoled, as to console;
Not so much to be understood as
To understand; not so much to be loved as to love;
For it is in giving that we receive;
It is in pardoning, that we are pardoned;
It is in dying, that we awaken to eternal life.

St. Francis of Assisi

20. Lovingkindness

The Lord hath appeared of old unto me, saying, Yea, I have loved thee with an everlasting love: therefore with lovingkindness have I drawn thee.

Jeremiah 31: 3

It is love, real divine love in our heart-depths which we need; happy, joyous, wise and good — the love which casts out hate and fear and transforms our whole outlook, our whole individuality and builds up and uplifts those around us.

Our adorable Lord is an infinity of our love, unbeginning, never ceasing and for ever an overflowing ocean of meekness, sweetness, delight, blessing and goodness, patience and mercy, and all this as so many streams breaking out of the abyss of universal love.

William Law

Love each other, says the Master.
If we each seek so to do,
We shall do it better, faster,
If He lives in me and you.

Olive V. Luff

He who kindles the spark of love in another's heart, will in the end be warmed by its fire.

My Commonplace Book

Lord, we thank thee for thy great love that will never fail us. May thy love for us strengthen our love for others.

21. Humility

He hath shewed thee, O man, what is good; and what doth the Lord require of thee, but to do justly, and to love mercy, and to walk humbly with thy God?

Micah 6: 8

Every man's humanity is unique; there is not another like it in the world, nor ever likely to be; therefore his power for good is unique. It is a little different from the next man's — not necessarily greater or nobler but different. It has a personality and flavour that can only be a product of one single soul, and only in return for its particular contribution to the totality of life has that man a right to declare — 'For my sake was the world created.' To enrich life, and to give it added colour, is man's need and man's justification.

Source unknown

O let me hear Thee speaking
In accents clear and still,
Above the storms of passion,
The murmurs of self-will;
O speak to reassure me,
To chasten or control;
O speak, and make me listen,
Thou Guardian of my soul.

J.E. Bode

Beloved Heavenly Father, thank you for our knowledge of the right ways of life. Help us to live so that all we do and all we say, may show that we are truly thine. How precious to us is the knowledge of thy presence; may our hearts ever be filled with thy peace. Praise be to thee, our Lord.

22. Faithfulness

Well done, thou good and faithful servant; thou hast been faithful over a few things, I will make thee ruler over many things: enter thou into the joy of thy Lord.

Matthew 25: 21, 23

These words were spoken by Jesus in his parable of the talents. A man travelled into a far country, called his servants and gave five talents to one, two to another and one to the third. 'Every man according to his ability.' Then took his journey. The one with the five and the one with two, traded and doubled them; but the third buried his lord's money. Later, the master returned and said 'Well done' to the two servants who had doubled the money but the last who had buried his talents in fear he reproved. God gives each one of us some gift to be used for him. Each one of us can do something — the youngest to the oldest. It is up to us to use the gift we have in the best way we can, knowing that God is with us.

I am only one, but I *am* one, I cannot do everything but I can do something and by the grace of God that 'something' will I do.

Source unknown

There's a glorious work before us,
  A work both great and grand;
Everyone to-day should join us,
  And help with heart and hand.

Charles Garrett

Lord, we thank thee for the talents that thou hast given us. Show us how to use them in thy service. Give us the wisdom, knowledge and power to fulfil thy will.

23. Joy

For, lo, the winter is past, ... the flowers appear on the earth; the time of the singing of birds is come, and the voice of the turtle is heard in our land; the fig tree putteth forth her green figs, and the vines with the tender grape give a good smell.
Song of Solomon 2:11-13

Joy of heart lies in the fact that every hour of life we can be dispelling shadows, we must *feel* joy before we can radiate it. The world is scintillating with gladness, if we only have eyes to see it. There is the joy of Nature and of Beauty. The joy of human companionship and spiritual fellowship; the joy of worship and communion with infinite Love; and the joy of partnership with infinite power. How can we be miserable?
Source unknown

How great is God Almighty,
Who has made all things well.
C.F. Alexander

O Lord of every lovely thing,
 The Maker of them all,
Who from the winter's gloomy wing
Doth shed the splendours of the spring,
 On Thy great name we call.

Not Thine alone, because from Thee
 Our life and breath we hold:
But Thine because in Christ we see
The grace that sets our spirits free,
 And for the truth makes bold.

R.W. Callin

24. Radiance

Thou hast put gladness in my heart, more than in the time that their corn and their wine increased. I will both lay me down in peace, and sleep: for thou, Lord, only makest me dwell in safety.
Psalm 4: 7,8

Love can turn every day things into something finer,
Love can turn life's small craft into a dream-starred liner,
Love can turn rain-swept streets into a land enthralling,
Love can turn simple acts into a great devotion.
Love can light up a face till it shines like a lovely vision,
Love can mend broken things so you can't even see the division,
Love can do all these things if only our hearts will let it,
Love can find one bright smile even when things are tragic,
For love is life's greatest gift — it's loving turned to magic.
Source unknown

I come all rejoicing,
Creation's joy voicing,
'Our Father in heaven is loving—all love.'
His heart's full of kindness,
A heart of love only,
The heart of the Godhead—our Father is he!
Basilea Schlink

O my Lord God, fill me continually with more and more love for thee and thy children everywhere.

25. Myself

I have put my trust in the Lord God. *Psalm 73: 28*

I have to live with myself and so
I want to be fit for myself to know,
I want to be able as days go by
Always to look myself in the eye.
I don't want to stand with the setting sun
And hate myself for the things I have done.
I want to go out with my head erect,
I want to deserve all men's respect.
And here in the struggle for fame and self
I want to be able to like myself.
I don't want to look at myself and know
That I'm bluster and bluff and empty show.
I see what others can never see,
I know what others can never know,
So whatever happens I want to be
Self-respecting and conscience free.

Source unknown

I know that the only way to live truly with joy and peace in
my heart, is continually to draw near to God and put my
complete trust in him.

For our Lord's sake, do all the good ye can,
To all the people ye can, by all the means ye can,
In all the places ye can, as long as ever ye can.
(Words on an old inscription at Shrewsbury)

*Lord, I am thy child and in thy strength and with thy love
in my heart I will aim to radiate thy love.*

26. Healing

Jesus saith unto her, Damsel, I say unto thee, Arise. And
straightway the damsel arose and walked.

Mark 5: 41, 42

Many miracles are told in the Bible. Here is a modern one.
Dorothy Kerin lived with her mother; on Sunday evening,
Feb. 17th, 1912, this miracle happened: Her mother with
a few friends gathered around Dorothy's bed thinking she
had died — her doctor had said she could not possibly live;
her heart and lungs had ceased to function; for the past
fortnight she had lain like a log and never moved; for five
years she had been confined to her bed; five hospitals had
declared she was incurable, doctors had confirmed this.
All hope of recovery had been given up on this particular
evening ... but was Dorothy Kerin dead? Her unconscious
spirit certainly was not, for she heard a 'Voice' telling her
to get up and walk ... she obeyed, threw back her
bedclothes and to the amazement of her mother and
friends got something to eat! It was midnight when she
returned to her bed and slept. Early in the morning, after
hearing the news, her doctor quickly arrived and to
demonstrate her recovery she ran upstairs and down.
Later Dorothy was 'told' to heal the sick and her work was
greatly blessed; for over fifty years she lived an active,
beautiful life. Many still recall that she was 'told' to build
a church; and 'The Church of Christ the Healer' adjoins
Burrswood, one of the Dorothy Kerin 'Homes of Healing',
Groombridge, Kent, where I stayed in 1975 and 1976.

Hear in this solemn evening hour,
And in thy mercy heal us all.

Henry Twells

27. Eventide

… we have a building of God, a house not made with hands, eternal in the heavens.   *2 Corinthians 5: 1*

You tell me I am getting old, you mix my house with me;
You're looking at the outside, that's all that most folk see.
The dweller in the little house is young and bright and gay,
Just starting on a life that lasts through long, eternal day.

These few short years can't make me old, I feel I'm in my
    youth,
Eternity lies just ahead, full life and joy and truth.
We will not fret to see this house grow shabby day by day,
But look ahead to our new Home which never will decay.

My house is getting ready in the Land beyond the sky,
Its Architect and Builder is my Saviour now on high;
But I rather think He's leaving the furnishing to me,
So it's 'treasure up in Heaven' I must store each day you
    see.

Beth Coombe Harris
(abridged)

Through all the changing scenes of life,
    In trouble and in joy,
The praises of my God shall still
    My heart and tongue employ.

Nahum Tate

Loving Heavenly Father, knowing your love will follow us all the days of our lives, may we never forget that whether we be young or old, we are your children; may our desire be to serve you with all our hearts. Fill our homes and our hearts with your peace so that at the last we shall dwell with you for ever.

28. Blessings

Thus saith the Lord ... Yea, I have loved thee with an everlasting love: therefore with lovingkindness have I drawn thee.   *Jeremiah 31: 2,3*

> Loved with the everlasting love,
> Led by grace that love to know;
> Spirit, breathing from above,
> Thou hast taught me it is so.
> O this full and perfect peace!
> O this transport all divine!
> In a love which cannot cease
> I am His, and He is mine.
>
>   *G. W. Robinson*

Could I with ink the ocean fill and were every blade of grass a quill; were the whole sky of parchment made and every man a scribe by trade, to write the love of God above, would drain the ocean dry; nor could the scroll contain the whole, though stretched from sky to sky.

                    Source unknown

> This, this is the God we adore,
> Our faithful, unchangeable Friend;
> Whose love is as great as His power,
> And neither knows measure nor end.
>
>   *Joseph Hart*

Our God and Father we love thee because thou lovest us and proved thy love in the gift of thy beloved Son; and hast shed in our hearts thy love by the gracious Holy Spirit. Help us to commend thy great love to others, day by day. For Jesus' sake.

                    John W. Newton

SECTION TWO — The Word of God

29. The Bible is unique

How exceedingly wonderful it is that you and I can possess the greatest treasure the world affords; the Bible is not one book but a whole library, 66 books, 39 in the Old Testament, 27 in the New Testament. We are able to buy a copy in our own language to read.

The earliest parts of the Bible were written getting on for 3,000 years ago and no part is less than 1,800 years. They were written in many lands from distant Babylon to Rome, by many authors. The Bible remains forever new because it is about personal relationships between men and women and their relationships with God. The Bible is the book of love for each other and love for God — this is timeless and forever. You and I are privileged 'to have and to hold' this, the greatest treasure to be possessed.

The supreme reason why the Bible is unique and forever indispensable is because it is literally the only source-book for the life, words and the teaching of Jesus. It is only in and through Jesus Christ that our relationship with our fellowmen is the relationship of love, and that our relationship with God is possible at all.

William Barclay

Almighty and most merciful God, who hast given us the Bible to be the revelation of Thy great love for us, grant that we be made strong for Thy service and filled with the true knowledge of Thee and Thy Son Jesus Christ. This we ask for Thy love's sake.

George Adam Smith

30. A Wonderful Discovery

Search the Scriptures.   *John 5: 39*
Put them in an earthen vessel, that they may continue
many days.   *Jeremiah 32: 14*

Skins and papyrus were the first materials used for
writing the Old Testament, and the New Testament at
first, until parchment came into use. Papyrus came from
a reed which may grow as tall as a man, and thicker than
his wrist. The pith was cut into long strips, some being
laid vertically and others horizontally; the sheets were
joined edge to edge to form a long strip with a handle at
each end. When read it was unrolled by one hand and
rolled up again with the other. Because of the humid
Palestine climate scrolls were stored in earthenware jars.

In 1947 a thrilling discovery was made near the Dead
Sea when a Bedouin youth, following his goat into a cave,
found jars bearing Isaiah's writings and many parts of
the Psalms, etc. This discovery led to others in nearby
caves. The two Isaiah scrolls are at least a thousand years
older than the most ancient Hebrew text previously
known. (I read of these things in the guidebook I bought
when I visited the unique 'Shrine of the Book and its
Scrolls' in Jerusalem in 1966, and also visited the
community headquarters of the sect of the Essenes, who
had for two centuries pursued a life of prayer and study
near these caves.) How wonderfully God works! Unseen
things come into view, and the lost is found.

*O Lord, how precious is thy Word! From days long past
to the present age, this Word, the world's greatest
treasure, becomes enlarged. May we ever search the
Scriptures, and find therein the great truths that bring us
to know the Way, the Truth and the Life.*

31. How the Bible came to England

In the beginning was the word, and the word was with God, and the word was God. In him was life.   John 1: 1, 4

How did the Bible and the Light of Christianity come to US? In 1804 the British and Foreign Bible Society was born ... all through a Welsh girl, who saved for 6 years to buy a Bible, then, after walking 25 miles barefoot over the mountains was told there were none for sale! Rev. T. Charles of Bala later told this story of Mary Jones at a Committee Meeting of the R.T.S. Thus was the society formed which has produced and circulated millions of scriptures in over 1,300 languages.

Go back earlier. Gregory, Bishop of Rome, in 597 saw Anglo-Saxon children being sold as slaves in the market place; sad to hear none knew of Christ, he sent Augustine to our country — with a copy of the Psalms. After this, beautiful manuscripts were written in monasteries — you can see some of these in the British Museum. Bede was later one of the many monks who devoted his life to translating parts of the Bible. He died when the last word of St. John's Gospel was completed, 735 A.D. Over a century later Alfred became king of Wessex. (His mother had taught him to read the Bible.) He declared that God's law is better than man's, and began his Book of Law with the Ten Commandments.

Wycliffe in the 14th century, then came Tyndale in the 16th, to whom we owe the translating of the New Testament and the first printing of it. 1538: a Royal proclamation stated that a Bible must be placed in every church in the land. In 1611 James I brought the Authorised version into existence. Recently our New English Bible was published, and many other translations have appeared.

Blessed Lord, we thank thee for the Bible, thy Word.

32. In the Beginning

In the beginning God created the heaven and the earth. And God said, Let there be light: and there was light. And God said, Let the waters under the heaven be gathered together unto one place, and let the dry land appear: and it was so. And God called the dry land earth; and the gathering together of the waters called he seas: and God saw that it was good. And God made two great lights; the greater light to rule the day, and the lesser light to rule the night: he made the stars also. And God said, Let the waters bring forth abundantly the moving creature that hath life, and the fowl that may fly above the earth. And God said, Let the earth bring forth the living creature after his kind: and it was so. And God said, Let us make man in our image, after our likeness: and let them have dominion over the fowl of the air, and over the cattle, and over all the earth, and over every creature that creepeth upon the earth.

So God created man in his own image, in the image of God created he him; male and female created he them. And God saw every thing that he had made, and behold, it was very good.

From Genesis 1

He makes the grass the hills adorn,
And clothes the smiling fields with corn;
The beasts with food His hands supply,
And the young ravens when they cry.

Isaac Watts

Come, divine Interpreter,
Bring us eyes Thy Book to read.

Charles Wesley

33. A Goodly Child

And there went a man of the house of Levi, and took to wife a daughter of Levi. And the woman conceived, and bare a son: and when she saw him that he was a goodly child, she hid him three months. And when she could no longer hide him, she took for him an ark of bulrushes, and daubed it with slime and with pitch, and put the child therein; and she laid it in the flags by the river's brink. And his sister stood afar off, to wit what would be done to him.

And the daughter of Pharaoh came down to wash herself at the river; and when she saw the ark among the flags, she sent her maid to fetch it. And when she had opened it, she saw the child: and, behold, the babe wept. And she had compassion on him, and said, This is one of the Hebrews' children. Then said his sister to Pharaoh's daughter, Shall I go and call to thee a nurse of the Hebrew women, that she may nurse the child for thee? And Pharaoh's daughter said to her, Go. And the maid went and called the child's mother. And the child grew, and she brought him to Pharaoh's daughter, and he became her son. And she called his name Moses, and she said, Because I drew him out of the water.

Exodus 2: 1-10

God's hand is my perpetual guard,
He guides me with His eye.

Isaac Watts

O Lord, in thy strength, and full of thy love, may we take the first step towards our goal — and go forward in faith, leaving the end in thy hands.

34. When Quiet in my House I sit

Hear, O Israel: the Lord our God is one Lord: and thou shalt love the Lord thy God with all thine heart, and with all thy soul, and with all thy might. And these words, which I command thee this day, shall be in thine heart: and thou shalt teach them diligently unto thy children, and shalt talk of them when thou sittest in thine house, and when thou walkest by the way, and when thou liest down, and when thou risest up. And thou shalt write them upon the posts of thy house, and on thy gates. And it shall be, when the Lord thy God shall have brought thee into the land which he sware unto thy fathers to give thee great and goodly cities, which thou buildedst not, and houses full of all good things, which thou filledst not, and wells digged, which thou diggedst not, vineyards and olive trees, which thou plantedst not; when thou shalt have eaten and be full; then beware lest thou forget the Lord thy God.

From Deuteronomy 6

Rising to sing my Saviour's praise,
　　Thee may I publish all day long;
And let Thy precious word of grace
　　Flow from my heart, and fill my tongue;
Fill all my life with purest love,
And join me to the Church above.

Charles Wesley

O God, teach us to obey thy will. Let thy Spirit flow like a river into our souls and cleanse us.

35. Entreat me not to leave thee

Elimelech, Naomi's husband, died; and she was left, and her two sons. And they took them wives of the women of Moab; the name of the one was Orpah, and the name of the other Ruth: and they dwelled there about ten years. And Mahlon and Chilion, her sons, died also both of them; and the woman was left of her two sons and her husband.

And Naomi said unto her two daughters in law, Go, return each to her mother's house: the Lord deal kindly with you, as ye have dealt with the dead, and with me. The Lord grant you that ye may find rest, each of you, in the house of her husband. Then she kissed them, and they lifted up their voice and wept. Orpah kissed her mother in law; but Ruth clave unto her. And she said, Behold, thy sister in law is gone back unto her people ... And Ruth said, Intreat me not to leave thee, or to return from following after thee: for whither thou goest, I will go; and where thou lodgest, I will lodge: thy people shall be my people, and thy God my God. Where thou diest, will I die, and there will I be buried: the Lord do so to me, and more also, if ought but death part thee and me.

Ruth 1: 3-5, 8-9, 14-17

Love is the key of life and death,
Of hidden heavenly mystery.

C.G. Rossetti

O Lord, so fill us with thy love that others too may be blessed, and be drawn to thee.

36. God speaks to Samuel

And it came to pass that at the time, when Eli was laid down in his place, and his eyes began to wax dim, that he could not see; and ere the lamp of God went out in the temple of the Lord, where the ark of God was, and Samuel was laid down to sleep; that the Lord called Samuel: and he answered, Here am I. And he ran unto Eli, and said, Here am I; for thou calledst me. And he said, I called not; lie down again. And he went and lay down. And the Lord called yet again, Samuel. And Samuel arose and went to Eli, and said, Here am I; for thou didst call me. And he answered, I called not, my son; lie down again. Now Samuel did not yet know the Lord, neither was the word of the Lord yet revealed unto him. And the Lord called Samuel again the third time. And he rose up and went to Eli, and said, Here am I: for thou didst call me. And Eli perceived that the Lord had called the child. Therefore Eli said unto Samuel, Go, lie down: and it shall be, if he call thee, that thou shalt say, Speak, Lord; for thy servant heareth. So Samuel went and lay down in his place. And the Lord came, and stood, and called as at other times, Samuel, Samuel. Then Samuel answered, Speak; for thy servant heareth.

1 Samuel 3: 2-10

O give me Samuel's mind,
  A sweet unmurmuring faith,
Obedient and resigned
  To Thee in life and death.

J.D. Burns

Lord, may I see the way for me.

37. What is Man?

O Lord our Lord, how excellent is thy name in all the earth! who hast set thy glory above the heavens. Out of the mouth of babes and sucklings hast thou ordained strength because of thine enemies, that thou mightest still the enemy and the avenger. When I consider thy heavens, the work of thy fingers, the moon and the stars which thou hast ordained; what is man, that thou art mindful of him? and the son of man, that thou visitest him? For thou hast made him a little lower than the angels, and hast crowned him with glory and honour. Thou madest him to have dominion over the works of thy hands; thou hast put all things under his feet: all sheep and oxen, yea, and the beasts of the field; the fowl of the air, and the fish of the sea, and whatsoever passeth through the paths of the seas. O Lord our Lord, how excellent is thy name in all the earth!

Psalm 8

Thine, Lord, we are, and ours Thou art;
  In us be all Thy goodness showed.
Renew, enlarge, and fill our heart
  With peace, and joy, and heaven, and God.

John Wesley

Lord, we thank thee for thy loving care, and for the prayers that thou hast answered. From much evil hast thou delivered us; we praise thee for thy safe keeping of us.

38. God's beauty everywhere

Lord, thou hast been our dwelling place in all generations. Before the mountains were brought forth, or ever thou hadst formed the earth and the world, even from everlasting to everlasting, thou art God. The days of our years are threescore years and ten; and if by reason of strength they be fourscore years, yet is their strength labour and sorrow; for it is soon cut off, and we fly away. So teach us to number our days, that we may apply our hearts unto wisdom. O satisfy us early with thy mercy; that we may rejoice and be glad all our days. Let thy work appear unto thy servants, and thy glory unto their children. And let the beauty of the Lord be upon us; and establish thou the work of our hands upon us; yea, the work of our hands establish thou it.

From Psalm 90

For each perfect gift of Thine
  To our race so freely given,
Graces human and divine,
  Flowers of earth and buds of heaven:
Gracious God, to Thee we raise
This our sacrifice of praise.

F.S. Pierpoint

Dear Lord, we do thank thee for so many lovely things: fresh air and sunshine; the fruits of the earth; for flowers so beautiful, and trees, birds — for kind neighbours and friends. We thank thee too for daily refreshment and renewal.

39. My Refuge and my Fortress

He that dwelleth in the secret place of the most High shall abide under the shadow of the Almighty. I will say of the Lord, He is my refuge and my fortress: my God; in him will I trust. Surely he shall deliver thee from the snare of the fowler, and from the noisome pestilence. He shall cover thee with his feathers, and under his wings shalt thou trust: his truth shall be thy shield and buckler. Thou shalt not be afraid for the terror by night; nor for the arrow that flieth by day; nor for the pestilence that walketh in darkness; nor for the destruction that wasteth at noonday. For he shall give his angels charge over thee, to keep thee in all thy ways.

Because he hath set his love upon me, therefore will I deliver him: I will set him on high, because he hath known my name. He shall call upon me, and I will answer him: I will be with him in trouble; I will deliver him, and honour him. With long life will I satisfy him, and shew him my salvation.

From Psalm 91

God is the refuge of His saints,
　When storms of sharp distress invade;
Ere we can offer our complaints,
　Behold Him present with His aid!

Isaac Watts

Lord, during the night watches there were many things on my mind. I give them all over to thee, knowing that thou wilt deal with them. My loved ones and I — we are all in thy keeping.

40. Hallelujah!

Bless the Lord, O my soul: and all that is within me, bless his holy name. Bless the Lord, O my soul, and forget not all his benefits: who forgiveth all thine iniquities; who healeth all thy diseases; who redeemeth thy life from destruction; who crowneth thee with loving-kindness and tender mercies; who satisfieth thy mouth with good things; so that thy youth is renewed like the eagle's. The Lord executeth righteousness and judgment for all that are oppressed. He made known his ways unto Moses, his acts unto the children of Israel. The Lord is merciful and gracious, slow to anger, and plenteous in mercy. He will not always chide: neither will he keep his anger for ever. He hath not dealt with us after our sins; nor rewarded us according to our iniquities. For as the heaven is high above the earth, so great is his mercy toward them that fear him. As far as the east is from the west, so far hath he removed our transgressions from us. Like as a father pitieth his children, so the Lord pitieth them that fear him. For he knoweth our frame; he remembereth that we are dust.

Psalm 103: 1-14

Father of mercies, in Thy Word
What endless glory shines!

Anne Steele

Thank you, Lord, for the gift of a new day; for the rest of the night, and for the strength to be up and about once more; for this time with thee before I face the duties of the day.

41. God sends a man

And there shall come forth a rod out of the stem of Jesse, and a Branch shall grow out of his roots: and the spirit of the Lord shall rest upon him, the spirit of wisdom and understanding, the spirit of counsel and might, the spirit of knowledge and of the fear of the Lord; and he shall not judge after the sight of his eyes, neither reprove after the hearing of his ears: but with righteousness shall he judge the poor, and reprove with equity for the meek of the earth: and he shall smite the earth with the rod of his mouth, and with the breath of his lips shall he slay the wicked. And righteousness shall be the girdle of his loins, and faithfulness the girdle of his reins. The wolf also shall dwell with the lamb, and the leopard shall lie down with the kid; and the calf and the young lion and the fatling together, and a little child shall lead them. They shall not hurt nor destroy in all my holy mountain: for the earth shall be full of the knowledge of the Lord, as the waters cover the sea.

From Isaiah 11: 1-6, 9

Fight we the fight with sorrow and sin,
   to set their captives free,
That the earth may be filled with the glory of God,
   as the waters cover the sea.

A.C. Ainger

Give me such love for thee, O God, and for men, as will blot out all hatred and bitterness.

Dietrich Bonhoëffer

42. Wait on the Lord

To whom then will ye liken me, or shall I be equal? saith the Holy One. Lift up your eyes on high, and behold who hath created these things, that bringeth out their host by number: he calleth them all by names by the greatness of his might, for that he is strong in power; not one faileth. Why sayest thou, O Jacob, and speakest, O Israel, My way is hid from the Lord, and my judgment is passed over from my God? Hast thou not known? hast thou not heard, that the everlasting God, the Lord, the Creator of the ends of the earth, fainteth not, neither is weary? there is no searching of his understanding. He giveth power to the faint; and to them that have no might he increaseth strength. Even the youths shall faint and be weary, and the young men shall utterly fall: but they that wait upon the Lord shall renew their strength; they shall mount up with wings as eagles; they shall run, and not be weary; and they shall walk, and not faint.

Isaiah 40: 25-31

True, 'tis a strait and thorny road,
And mortal spirits tire and faint;
But they forget the mighty God
That feeds the strength of every saint.

Isaac Watts

Set a watch, O Lord, before my mouth; keep the door of my lips ... mine eyes are unto thee, O God: in thee is my trust.

Psalm 141: 3, 8

43. Your Father knoweth

When thou prayest, thou shalt not be as the hypocrites are: for they love to pray standing in the synagogues and in the corners of the streets, that they may be seen of men. Verily I say unto you, They have their reward. But thou, when thou prayest, enter into thy closet, and when thou hast shut thy door, pray to thy Father which is in secret; and thy Father which seeth in secret shall reward thee openly. But when ye pray, use not vain repetitions, as the heathen do: for they think that they shall be heard for their much speaking. Be not ye therefore like unto them: for your Father knoweth what things ye have need of, before ye ask him.

After this manner therefore pray ye: Our Father which art in heaven, hallowed by thy name. Thy kingdom come, thy will be done in earth, as it is in heaven. Give us this day our daily bread. And forgive us our debts, as we forgive our debtors. And lead us not into temptation, but deliver us from evil: For thine is the kingdom, and the power, and the glory, for ever.

Matthew 6: 5-13

Jesu, my single eye
    Be fixed on Thee alone:
Thy name be praised on earth, on high;
    Thy will by all be done.

Charles Wesley

Our Father, we pray thee, send into our hearts and into the hearts of men everywhere the Spirit of our Lord Jesus Christ.

44. Be not anxious

Take no thought for your life, what ye shall eat, or what ye shall drink; nor yet for your body, what ye shall put on. Is not the life more than meat, and the body than raiment? Behold the fowls of the air: for they sow not, neither do they reap, nor gather into barns; yet your heavenly Father feedeth them. Are ye not much better than they? Which of you by taking thought can add one cubit unto his stature? And why take ye thought for raiment? Consider the lilies of the field, how they grow; they toil not, neither do they spin. And yet I say unto you, that even Solomon in all his glory was not arrayed like one of these. Wherefore, if God so clothe the grass of the field, which today is, and tomorrow is cast into the oven, shall he not much more clothe you, O ye of little faith? Therefore take no thought, saying, What shall we eat? or, What shall we drink? or, Wherewithal shall we be clothed? for your heavenly Father knoweth that ye have need of all these things.

Matthew 6: 25-32

Thou art the Way, the Truth, the Life;
  Grant us that way to know,
That Truth to keep, that Life to win,
  Whose joys eternal flow.

G. W. Doane

Yesterday you helped me, Lord. Today I praise your name. For I know tomorrow you will help me just the same!

45. The men who just kept on

And they come unto him, bringing one sick of the palsy, which was borne of four. And when they could not come nigh unto him for the press, they uncovered the roof where he was: and when they had broken it up, they let down the bed wherein the sick of the palsy lay. When Jesus saw their faith, he said unto the sick of the palsy, Son, thy sins be forgiven thee. But there were certain of the scribes sitting there, and reasoning in their hearts, why doth this man thus speak blasphemies? who can forgive sins but God only? And immediately when Jesus perceived in his spirit that they so reasoned within themselves, he said unto them, Why reason ye these things in your hearts? Whether is it easier to say to the sick of the palsy, Thy sins be forgiven thee; or to say, Arise, and take up thy bed, and walk? But that ye may know that the Son of man hath power on earth to forgive sins, (he saith to the sick of the palsy,) I say unto thee, Arise, and take up thy bed, and go thy way into thine house. And immediately he arose, took up the bed, and went forth before them all; insomuch that they were all amazed, and glorified God, saying, We never saw it on this fashion.

Mark 2: 3-12

Wouldst Thou the body's health restore,
 And not regard the sin-sick soul?
The sin-sick soul Thou lov'st much more,
 And surely Thou shalt make it whole.

Charles Wesley

Lord, may we too have a tremendous love of souls and a great faith in thy power and love.

46. Sheep or Goat: which shall I be?

When the Son of man shall come in his glory, and all the holy angels with him, then shall he sit upon the throne of his glory: and before him shall be gathered all nations: and he shall separate them one from another, as a shepherd divideth his sheep from the goats: and he shall set the sheep on his right hand, but the goats on the left. Then shall the King say unto them on his right hand, Come, ye blessed of my Father, inherit the kingdom prepared for you from the foundation of the world: for I was an hungred, and ye gave me meat: I was thirsty, and ye gave me drink: I was a stranger, and ye took me in: naked, and ye clothed me: I was sick, and ye visited me: I was in prison, and ye came unto me. Then shall the righteous answer him, saying, Lord, when saw we thee an hungred, and fed thee? Or thirsty, and gave thee drink? When saw we thee a stranger, and took thee in? Or naked, and clothed thee? Or when saw we thee sick, or in prison, and came unto thee? And the King shall answer and say unto them, Verily I say unto you, Inasmuch as ye have done it unto one of the least of these my brethren, ye have done it unto me.

Matthew 25: 31-40

In a service which Thy will appoints
  There are no bounds for me;
And a life of self-renouncing love
  Is a life of liberty.

A.L. Waring

Dear Lord, give me more love, so that I may serve thee better in the years that are left to me. Inspire all I do so that through thee I may be a blessing to all whom I meet.

47. The great Visitation

And there were in the same country shepherds abiding in the field, keeping watch over their flock by night. And, lo, the angel of the Lord came upon them, and the glory of the Lord shone round about them, and they were sore afraid. And the angel said unto them, Fear not: for, behold, I bring you good tidings of great joy, which shall be to all people. For unto you is born this day in the city of David a Saviour, which is Christ the Lord. And this shall be a sign unto you; Ye shall find the babe wrapped in swaddling clothes, lying in a manger. And suddenly there was with the angel a multitude of the heavenly host praising God, and saying, Glory to God in the highest, and on earth peace, good will toward men. And it came to pass, as the angels were gone away from them into heaven, the shepherds said one to another, Let us now go even unto Bethlehem and see this thing which is come to pass, which the Lord hath made known to us. And they came with haste, and found Mary, and Joseph, and the babe lying in a manger. And when they had seen it, they made known abroad the saying which was told them concerning this child. But Mary kept all these things, and pondered them in her heart.

Luke 2: 8-17, 19

Once in royal David's city
 Stood a lowly cattle-shed,
Where a mother laid her baby
 In a manger for His bed.

C.F. Alexander

Help me, dear Lord, to keep all these precious things in my heart. May a great abundance of thy love flow out upon all whom I may meet.

48. Abide with me

And they drew nigh unto the village, whither they went: and he made as though he would have gone further. But they constrained him, saying, Abide with us: for it is toward evening, and the day is far spent. And he went in to tarry with them. And it came to pass, as he sat at meat with them, he took bread, and blessed it, and brake, and gave to them. And their eyes were opened, and they knew him; and he vanished out of their sight. And they said one to another, Did not our heart burn within us... while he opened to us the scriptures? And they rose up the same hour, and returned to Jerusalem, and found the eleven gathered together, and them that were with them, saying, the Lord is risen indeed, and hath appeared to Simon. And they told what things were done in the way, and how he was known of them in breaking of bread.

Luke 24: 28-35

Abide with me; fast falls the eventide;
The darkness deepens; Lord, with me abide!
When other helpers fail, and comforts flee,
Help of the helpless, O abide with me.

H.F. Lyte

O Lord, I long to be thy true child, to be fully thine. May I grow in knowledge and in love continually, for thee and for others. Cleanse thou my thoughts and make me pure.

49. The Word of God

In the beginning was the Word, and the Word was with God, and the Word was God. The same was in the beginning with God. All things were made by him; and without him was not anything made that was made. In him was life; and the life was the light of men. And the light shineth in darkness, and the darkness comprehended it not. There was a man sent from God, whose name was John. The same came for a witness, to bear witness of the Light, that all men through him might believe. He was not that Light, but was sent to bear witness of that Light. That was the true Light, which lighteth every man that cometh into the world. He was in the world, and the world was made by him, and the world knew him not. He came unto his own, and his own received him not. But as many as received him, to them gave he power to become the sons of God, even to them that believe on his name: which were born, not of blood, nor of the will of the flesh, nor of the will of man, but of God. And the Word was made flesh, and dwelt among us, (and we beheld his glory, the glory as of the only begotten of the Father,) full of grace and truth.

John 1: 1-14

Of the Father's love begotten
 Ere the worlds began to be,
He is Alpha and Omega,
 He the source, the ending, He,
Of the things that are, that have been,
And that future years shall see,
 Evermore and evermore.

A.C. Prudentius, tr. J.M. Neale

50. The Good Shepherd

I am the door: by me if any man shall enter in, he shall be saved, and shall go in and out, and find pasture. I am the good shepherd: the good shepherd giveth his life for the sheep. But he that is an hireling, and not the shepherd, whose own the sheep are not, seeth the wolf coming, and leaveth the sheep, and fleeth: and the wolf catcheth them, and scattereth the sheep. The hireling fleeth, because he is an hireling, and careth not for the sheep. I am the good shepherd, and know my sheep, and am known of mine. As the Father knoweth me, even so know I the Father: and I lay down my life for the sheep. And other sheep I have, which are not of this fold: them also I must bring, and they shall hear my voice; and there shall be one fold, and one shepherd. Therefore doth my Father love me, because I lay down my life, that I might take it again. I have power to lay it down, and I have power to take it again.

John 10: 9-18

The King of love my Shepherd is,
  Whose goodness faileth never;
I nothing lack if I am His
  And He is mine for ever.

H.W. Baker

Lord God, we pray that we may more and more practise thy law of love, seek to follow Jesus' teaching, and walk in thy way and do thy will.

51. Serve one another

Now before the feast of the passover, when Jesus knew that his hour was come that he should depart out of this world unto the Father, having loved his own which were in the world, he loved them unto the end. And supper being ended, the devil having now put into the heart of Judas Iscariot, Simon's son, to betray him; Jesus knowing that the Father had given all things into his hands, and that he was come from God, and went to God; he riseth from supper, and laid aside his garments; and took a towel, and girded himself. After that he poureth water into a basin, and began to wash the disciples' feet, and to wipe them with the towel wherewith he was girded. So after he had washed their feet, and had taken his garments, and was set down again, he said unto them, Know ye what I have done to you? Ye call me Master and Lord: and ye say well; for so I am. If I then, your Lord and Master, have washed your feet; ye also ought to wash one another's feet. For I have given you an example, that ye should do as I have done to you.

John 13: 1-5, 12-15

Heaven's arches rang
When the angels sang,
Proclaiming Thy royal degree;
But of lowly birth
Cam'st Thou, Lord, on earth,
And in great humility:

O come to my heart, Lord Jesus;
There is room in my heart for Thee.

E.E.S. Elliott

52. Love one another

If ye abide in me, and my words abide in you, ye shall ask what ye will, and it shall be done unto you. Herein is my Father glorified, that ye bear much fruit; so shall ye be my disciples. As the Father hath loved me, so have I loved you: continue ye in my love. If ye keep my commandments, ye shall abide in my love; even as I have kept my Father's commandments, and abide in his love. These things have I spoken unto you, that my joy might remain in you, and that your joy might be full. This is my commandment, That ye love one another, even as I have loved you. Greater love hath no man than this, that a man lay down his life for his friends. Ye are my friends, if ye do whatsoever I command you. Henceforth I call you not servants; for the servant knoweth not what his lord doeth: but I have called you friends. These things I command you, that ye love one another.

John 15: 7-15, 17

There is no love like the love of Jesus,
  Never to fade or fall
Till into the fold of the peace of God
  He has gathered us all.
Jesu's love, precious love,
  Boundless and pure and free;
Oh, turn to that love, weary wandering soul,
  Jesus pleadeth with thee!

W.E. Littlewood

O Lord, I give myself to thee. Thou art love, so all the love I am capable of, all the love thou hast put into my heart, is thine.

53. The day the Spirit came

And when the day of Pentecost was fully come, they were all with one accord in one place. And suddenly there came a sound from heaven as of a rushing mighty wind, and it filled all the house where they were sitting. And there appeared unto them cloven tongues like as of fire, and it sat upon each of them. And they were all filled with the Holy Ghost, and began to speak with other tongues, as the Spirit gave them utterance. And there were dwelling at Jerusalem Jews, devout men, out of every nation under heaven. Now when this was noised abroad, the multitude came together, and were confounded, because that every man heard them speak in his own language. And they were all amazed and marvelled, saying one to another, Behold, are not all these which speak Galileans? And how hear we every man in our own tongue, wherein we were born?

Acts 2: 1-8

When shall I hear the inward voice
  Which only faithful souls can hear?
Pardon, and peace, and heavenly joys
  Attend the promised Comforter:
Oh come! and righteousness divine,
  And Christ, and all with Christ, are mine.

Charles Wesley

Come down, O Love Divine,
Seek Thou this soul of mine.

Tr. R.F. Littledale

54. I am persuaded

We know that all things work together for good to them that love God, to them who are the called according to his purpose. What shall we then say to these things? If God be for us, who can be against us? He that spared not his own Son, but delivered him up for us all, how shall he not with him also freely give us all things? Who shall lay any thing to the charge of God's elect? It is God that justifieth. Who is he that condemneth? It is Christ that died, yea rather, that is risen again, who is even at the right hand of God, who also maketh intercession for us. Who shall separate us from the love of Christ? shall tribulation, or distress, or persecution, or famine, or nakedness, or peril, or sword? Nay, in all these things we are more than conquerors, through him that loved us. For I am persuaded that neither death, nor life, nor angels, nor principalities, nor powers, nor things present, nor things to come, nor height, nor depth, nor any other creature, shall be able to separate us from the love of God, which is in Christ Jesus our Lord.

Romans 8: 28, 31-35, 37-39

From Him who loves me now so well
  What power my soul shall sever?
Shall life or death? shall earth or hell?
  No! I am His for ever.

J.G. Small

Lord, I know that NOTHING can separate me from thy love. I praise and thank thee. Strengthen thou me in that great love.

55. The greatest of these

Though I speak with the tongues of men and of angels, and have not charity, I am become as sounding brass, or a tinkling cymbal. And though I have the gift of prophecy, and understand all mysteries, and all knowledge; and though I have all faith, so that I could remove mountains, and have not charity, I am nothing. And though I bestow all my goods to feed the poor, and though I give my body to be burned, and have not charity, it profiteth me nothing. Charity suffereth long, and is kind; charity envieth not; charity vaunteth not itself, is not puffed up, doth not behave itself unseemly, seeketh not her own, is not easily provoked, thinketh no evil; rejoiceth not in iniquity, but rejoiceth in the truth; beareth all things, believeth all things, hopeth all things, endureth all things. Charity never faileth: but whether there be prophecies, they shall fail, whether there be tongues, they shall cease; whether there be knowledge, it shall vanish away. For now we see through a glass, darkly; but then face to face: now I know in part; but then shall I know even as also I am known. And now abideth faith, hope, charity, these three; but the greatest of these is charity.

1 Corinthians 13: 1-8, 12-13

Happy the heart where graces reign,
  Where love inspires the breast;
Love is the brightest of the train
  And perfects all the rest.

Isaac Watts

O dear Lord, may thy love cleanse me, physically, mentally and spiritually.

56. The new life in Christ

If ye then be risen with Christ, seek those things which are above, where Christ sitteth on the right hand of God. Set your affection on things above, not on things on the earth. For ye are dead, and your life is hid with Christ in God. When Christ, who is our life, shall appear, then shall ye also appear with him in glory. Put on therefore, as the elect of God, holy and beloved, bowels of mercies, kindness, humbleness of mind, meekness, longsuffering; forbearing one another, and forgiving one another, if any man have a quarrel against any: even as Christ forgave you, so also do ye. And above all these things put on charity, which is the bond of perfectness. And let the peace of God rule in your hearts, to the which also ye are called in one body; and be ye thankful. Let the word of Christ dwell in you richly in all wisdom; teaching and admonishing one another in psalms and hymns and spiritual songs, singing with grace in your hearts to the Lord. And whatsoever ye do in word or deed, do all in the name of the Lord Jesus, giving thanks to God and the Father by him.

Colossians 3: 1-4, 12-17

Ye faithful souls who Jesus know,
  If risen indeed with Him ye are
Superior to the joys below,
  His resurrection's power declare.

Charles Wesley

Lord, I have done many things I ought not to have done, and left undone many things I ought to have done: but the love and faith I have for thee have kept me from many other sins I could have committed! Praise to thee for the many friends who have kept me near to thee.

57. The Way of Love

Beloved, let us love one another: for love is of God; and every one that loveth is born of God, and knoweth God. He that loveth not knoweth not God: for God is love. Beloved, if God so loved us, we ought also to love one another. No man hath seen God at any time. If we love one another, God dwelleth in us, and his love is perfected in us. And we have seen and do testify that the Father sent the Son to be the Saviour of the world. Whosoever shall confess that Jesus is the Son of God, God dwelleth in him, and he in God. God is love; and he that dwelleth in love, dwelleth in God, and God in him. Herein is our love made perfect, that we may have boldness in the day of judgment: because as he is, so are we in this world. There is no fear in love; but perfect love casteth out fear: because fear hath torment. He that feareth is not made perfect in love. We love him, because he first loved us. If a man say, I love God, and hateth his brother, he is a liar: for he that loveth not his brother whom he hath seen, how can he love God whom he hath not seen? And this commandment have we from him, That he who loveth God love his brother also.

1 John 4: 7-8, 11, 12, 14-21

God is love: His mercy brightens
All the path in which we rove.

John Bowring

Lord God Almighty, come into our hearts and souls and minds and enrich us. May we joyously do thy will.

58. Glory — for ever!

And I saw a new heaven and a new earth: for the first heaven and the first earth were passed away; and there was no more sea. And I John saw the holy city, new Jerusalem, coming down from God out of heaven, prepared as a bride adorned for her husband. And I heard a great voice out of heaven saying, Behold, the tabernacle of God is with men, and he will dwell with them, and they shall be his people, and God himself shall be with them and be their God. And God shall wipe away all tears from their eyes; and there shall be no more death, neither sorrow, nor crying, neither shall there be any more pain: for the former things are passed away. And he that sat upon the throne said, Behold, I make all things new. And he said unto me, Write: for these words are true and faithful. And he said unto me, It is done. I am Alpha and Omega, the beginning and the end. I will give unto him that is athirst of the fountain of the water of life freely. He that overcometh shall inherit all things; and I will be his God, and he shall be my son. His servants shall serve him: and they shall see his face; and his name shall be in their foreheads. And there shall be no night there; and they need no candle, neither light of the sun; for the Lord God giveth them light: and they shall reign for ever and ever.

Revelation 21: 1-7; 22: 3-5

Jerusalem, Jerusalem,
   God grant me once to see
Thy endless joys, and of the same
   Partaker aye to be.

F.B.P., 16th or 17th cent.

So teach us to number our days, that we may apply our hearts unto wisdom.

Psalm 90: 12